Cadron Creek

Cadron Creek
A Photographic Narrative

by Lil Junas

The Ozark Society Foundation
Little Rock, Arkansas

With support from the Arkansas Endowment for the Humanities
and the Faulkner County Historical Society

Library of Congress Catalog Card Number: 79-90495.
International Standard Book Number: 0 912456-05-1.

Photographs, text and design by Lil Junas.

Typesetting by the Conway Printing Company,
    Conway, Ark.
Printing and binding by Kingsport Press,
    Kingsport, Tenn.

Printed in the United States of America.

**Dedicated
to the preservation
of God's design of nature**

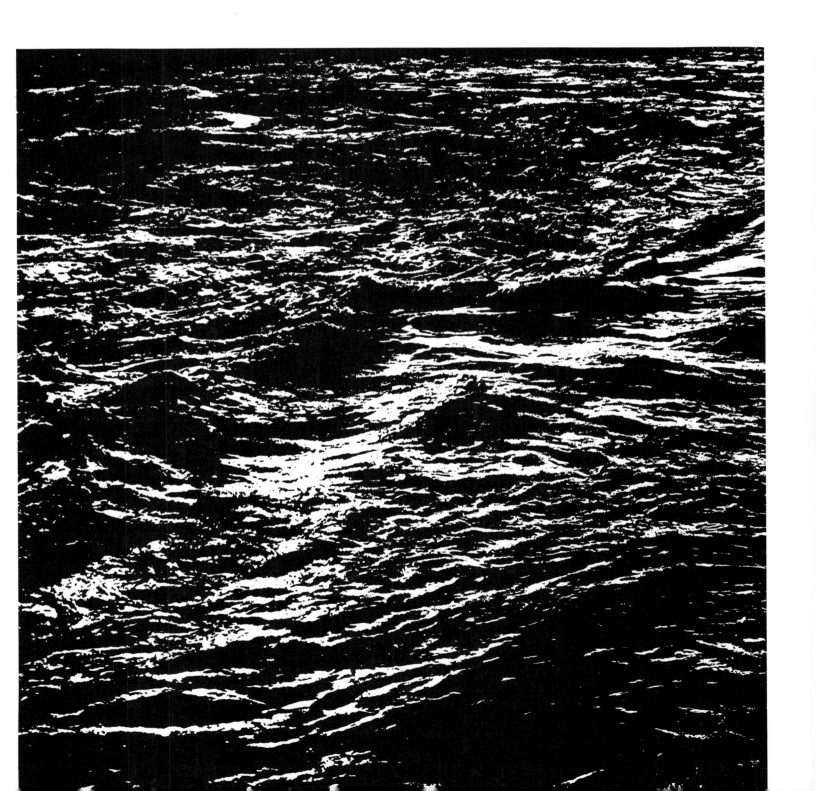

Recognitions

Without the interest and cooperation of many persons, this book never could have been completed:

To Grace Kuikman whose ideas and many hours of editing in the early stages of preparing the manuscript were invaluable;

To Mary Virginia Ferguson for her time and untiring efforts in preparing grant proposals, contacting supporting organizations and individuals, making suggestions and helping in so many ways;

To Dick and Laurna Tallman for final editing and consultation;

To Bob Fisher for his patience, moral support and direction as chairman of the Ozark Society Foundation;

To Alice Andrews with whom I canoed the Cadron for the first time and to my many other friends in the Ozark Society and the Save the Cadron group who accompanied me on several float trips and whose interest in the creek and in this book was an incentive.

To June Prange for editorial assistance;

To Pete Sherrill for reviewing the oral history aspects of the manuscript;

To Mina Marsh of the Arkansas Natural Heritage Commission, Leah Sylar and Anthony Dube of the Arkansas Endowment for the Humanities, and the Faulkner County Historical Society for their confidence in and support of this project;

To my family who, although miles from Arkansas, understood my efforts and concerns and offered encouragement;

To J. Clifton, Mavis and Margaret Chapman; Venice and Darse Joyner; Robert Mode; Myrtle, James and John Lane; J. D. Pratt; George Glover; Albert Presley; Derwayne Battles; Victor Halter; Tip Reynolds Davidson; Orphelia Mallett Garrett; Mrs. Cotton Reynolds; Bob Fugatt; Foye Mae Fugatt Bane and so many others who gave of their time to share their experiences of living along and enjoying the Cadron.

Prologue

The morning was cool and fresh with the fragrance of spring blossoms and new plant growth. Beyond the tiny leaf buds on the trees, the sky was cloudless. Anxious to get moving, I put my camera box and bucket of food and film in the canoe. My partner tossed in a few cushions. We were off—my first encounter with Cadron Creek. Only the water dripping from each paddle stroke broke the silence as we glided through the calm green water.

Soon, however, gurgling water alerted us to rapids beyond our view. We approached the curve slowly and aimed the bow at the "V" atop the waves. Our canoe took them with ease, and our excited shouts rang out with every wave we crashed. The creek was about 30 feet wide at this spot on the North Fork, and the water was deep enough to carry our canoe swiftly over the rocks.

For the next few minutes we paddled steadily through a long pool, with wildflowers and birds greeting us along the way. Emerald mosses and patches of orange and yellow crustose lichens gave an elegant touch to the bluffs. Streamlets coming from crevices in the layered sandstone formations enticed us to explore further. We climbed one pinnacle and beheld the panorama of the creek behind us and the valley and hills we were about to traverse. As we rested on the summit, the horizon in the east slowly exposed the sun which painted the tips of trees and bluffs in pastels. I was eager to see what lay ahead, so we returned quickly to the creek.

As we continued downstream, we passed a young couple sitting on a large flat rock near the water's edge and two older women in wide-brim sunbonnets fishing from folding chairs on a sandy bank. "Catching anything?" I asked. "Oh, a few," answered one, lifting a string of bass from the water. A hawk, silhouetted against the sky, escorted us about a half mile downstream, sailing back and forth across the creek, occasionally lighting on a high branch.

Another time, while hiking along the upper stretches of the East Fork of the Cadron, my reverence for the creek environment had renewed my bond with the outdoors. The intimate beauty had grown incredibly as I walked farther up the creek. It was comforting to experience the environment of the early settlers, an unspoiled habitat of small wild animals and birds, with no evidence of commercial or industrial development. A feeling of freedom—a feeling of owning a share of the sounds of the creek's current and the sights of the faunal spectrum—grew in me.

My acquaintance with the stately tupelo gum trees had hardly prepared me for the mysterious, bayou-like setting further upstream where the gnarled gums dominated the creek, dividing its current into a maze of channels. Blossoming wild plum trees perched atop the bluffs like bursts of fluffy clouds. The shocking pink of redbuds accented the greens and grays of the brush. The saxifrages and May apples already were responding to the call of spring.

The following winter I retraced my route along the East Cadron. The varied hues of the blooming flowers and trees were gone, but the silver cascade of ice on the bluffs and the ringlets of ice beads dressing the willow bushes and tupelos were a sight worth the journey. That day I met a young fellow returning home from hunting. A squirrel hung from his belt. The only other creatures I saw were a chipmunk scampering around the rocks and a lizard circling a tree trunk.

Robert L. Gatewood in *Faulkner County, Arkansas 1778-1964* refers to the largest stream in the county as "The Great Cadron Creek." For the farmers who live along the creek and for others who come to enjoy its resources, the Cadron is still "The Great Cadron Creek"—the pride of Central Arkansas. Meandering through hills and bluffs, marshes and lowlands, the Cadron makes a twisting descent in its quest for the Arkansas River. Along its capricious route, young and old alike have been enticed by its kaleidoscopic grandeur, its diverse moods.

This book is a photographic narration of Cadron Creek, accompanied by the words of those living within the range of its ripples—people who understand the creek and are committed to its preservation. Years of human experience compose the story of Cadron Creek. In these pages are reflected how the Cadron has made the lives of these people a little more fulfilling, a little more exciting. It is my hope that this book will help to make more enjoyable what we already enjoy.

Contents

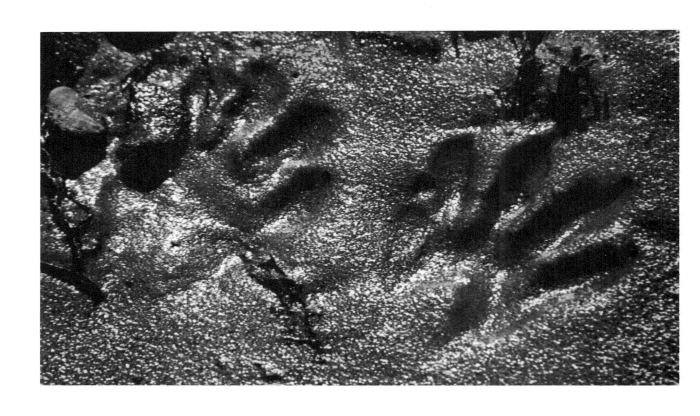

CADRON CREEK
—Its Name
—Its History
—Its Location

Blockhouse at Cadron Settlement Park

Its Name

The selection of the name "Cadron" has been attributed to various origins, none ever verified. One speculation is that the word derives from the Kidron Valley in Jerusalem, but although the sound of the name is similar, the reason for the connection is unknown. Another is that the name is a corruption of the French word "quatre," meaning four. Cadron Creek enters the Arkansas River near the four corners of four land sections. The theory is that the early English settlers had French maps with the word "quatre" marked where the lines of the four sections came together.

Knowing no French, the English-speaking Americans, trying to pronounce "quatre" came up with Cadron. This theory, however, is questionable since "quatre" should be pronounced "katr," and someone not knowing French likely would say "kwatre" which doesn't twist into Cadron. The French called the first Cadron settlement "Quadrant" because it was in these four sections.

The most likely explanation is that traders, who were sent to the Arkansas River area in 1762 by Capt. Charles Cadron from St. Phillipe in Canada, named the

creek for their captain. Whatever the origin, the early settlers evidently liked the name and, according to historical sources, Cadron Town (Settlement), Cadron Cove, Cadron Ridge, Cadron Gap and Cadron Valley were named after the creek.

Cadron Town no longer exists, and Cadron Cove was renamed Martinville after Capt. W. W. Martin, a wealthy bachelor who, with his brother J. D. Martin, owned a large hotel at Pinnacle Springs when that community was a prosperous resort on the Cadron in the late 1800's.

Its History

One of the early explorers of the Cadron Creek area was John Standlee who visited from 1778-80. His sons William, David and John and a son-in-law John C. Benedict came to the area from Missouri in 1811 to find home sites. As recorded in *Faulkner Facts and Fiddlings* by Ted R. Worley (1961) and in *Source Readings in Arkansas History* by Earl Leroy Higgins (1964), Benedict wrote in 1818 that they left Missouri for the "savage wild wilderness" of Arkansas, with pack horses, camp equipment, guns and ammunition, "harrassed and tormented by the savages and wild beasts. On the route we passed but one house from Little Red River to the mouth of the Cadron. . .and that was a small hut on the headwaters. . .at Frederick's Lick, where lived four brothers by the name of Wyley. . . These men were but little better than savages. Followed hunting. Had no farm and never had a garden. At the mouth of Cadron Creek we found a large block house built as a refuge from the hostile Osage Indians." The block house also was a trading center operated by John McElmurry, an agent for Frederick Notrebe, a wealthy merchant and trader at Arkansas Post.

Benedict and his brothers-in-law encamped on the bluff of Cadron Ridge. They built three small cabins and lived off buffalos, bears, elks, deer and turkeys.

"The Osage were bitter enemies to the few white settlers who were scattered from 20 to 50 miles apart in small groups of two or three families," Benedict's report continued. None of these had cultivated a hill of corn or even a garden patch—and were subsisting entirely on wild game. William and John Standlee with Thomas Burrows had begun a saw mill and grist mill but we still found no farms or any corn."

Cadron Town, established in 1811 near the mouth of the Cadron at the Arkansas River, was the first settlement on the creek. The site of the territorial capitol in 1820 before it moved to Little Rock the following year, Cadron Town also was the county seat of Pulaski County from 1820-21 and the county seat of Conway County from 1825-31. The first of many grist mills on the Cadron was built here, with most of the flour and grain being shipped via the Arkansas River. The first bridge across Cadron Creek, a 70-yard span, also was built at Cadron Town in 1827. Prior to this time, the miry creek bottom and high banks often made it impossible for wagons to ford.

The popularity of Cadron Town in 1819 was described in *Arkansas* (1947) by John Gould Fletcher: "On his way eastward and southward down the Arkansas River, Thomas Nuttall recorded his disgust at the 'dram-drinking, jockeying and gambling' crowd already collecting at Cadron in the two-room log tavern recently set up there. A considerable concourse of travelers and some emigrants began to make their appearance in this imaginary town."

The thriving river town, whose population once was 1,888, began to decline after the completion of the Little Rock-Fort Smith Railroad in 1872. River traffic, on which Cadron Town depended, gradually gave way to the rails. The town of Conway began to grow along the railroad and soon became the county seat and trade center.

In 1976 Cadron Settlement Park was established near the original site of Cadron Town. A blockhouse was erected during the following two years by the Conway Chamber of Commerce and the Faulkner County Historical Society in cooperation with the Army Corps of Engineers. The park's nature trail begins near the spring which served as the main source of water for the pioneers. The 7,500-foot trail winds adjacent to the eroded road bed of the former Butterfield Stage Line on the old mail route from Memphis to San Francisco. A low water bridge on the trail spans the ravine at the former grist mill site. Otherwise, no physical evidence remains of the passage of the early settlers through the area. Only the land use—still primarily agricultural—has remained essentially unchanged.

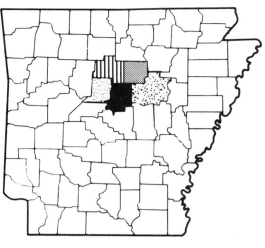

The Cadron flows through or touches five counties: clockwise from Faulkner (black), Conway, Van Buren, Cleburne, White.

State of Arkansas

Its Location

CADRON CREEK is a confluence of three branches: the North Fork, the East Fork and the West Fork. It flows through or touches five counties in Central Arkansas: Cleburne, White, Van Buren, Faulkner and Conway.

The NORTH FORK is the longest branch, flowing about 75 miles. Originating in Cleburne County southwest of Greers Ferry near the Old Cherokee Indian Boundary Line, it meanders southwest through Bettis and Pryor Mountains, turns east to meet the West Fork near the Cleburne - Van Buren - Faulkner borders, then continues in a southwesterly direction across Faulkner County.

Skirting the steep precipices of Batesville Mountain in northwestern Faulkner County, the North Fork cuts through a long section of high bluffs and pinnacles near Pinnacle Springs. It finally forms the Faulkner-Conway line before heading south toward the Arkansas River.

The EAST FORK starts in White County about one mile north of Highway 36 near Plants Chapel. About 50 miles long, it flows west across Faulkner County through hilly country, past Bluff, Mosely, White Oak and Bailey Mountains in its upper reaches. Continuing

through Cadron Valley, the East Fork drops abruptly as it approaches the lowlands, winding between Dunn Hill and North Cadron Ridge on its final descent to meet its sister fork on the Faulkner-Conway border about three miles north of Interstate 40. Most of the East Fork is in Faulkner County.

The WEST FORK is about 15 miles in length. Starting in Cleburne County about one-half mile from Highway 5, the West Fork enters Van Buren County where it joins the North Fork just north of Highway 124 about three miles west of Quitman. The West Fork is the only branch of the Cadron that does not enter Faulkner County.

Most of the history of Cadron Creek—and the livelihood and recreation it has provided—has flourished along the North and East Forks. Since these forks flow through such different terrains, have such distinct characteristics, and are scattered by as many as 25 miles, they appear to be different creeks.

More than 40 tributaries, formed from spring-fed streams and drainage, feed the Cadron. Among the main tributaries of the North Fork are Cove Creek, Batesville Creek, Cypress Creek and

Caney Creek. The main tributaries of the East Fork are Clear Creek, Black Fork and Cedar Branch. Many of the tributaries carry family names: Pierce, Taylor, Jackson, Ward, Cunningham, Mecum, Shelton, Addler, Blakey, Potter, Jones, Jacks, DeBerry and King.

Except for the weir near the mouth of the creek, the Cadron has about 140 free-flowing miles, most of them in Faulkner County.

As a fishing stream, the Cadron has a good rating. The Arkansas Game and Fish Commission in 1977 listed the East Cadron fish population at 58 percent game fish and the North Cadron at 41 percent, "suggesting a rather high quality fishing stream."

The Cadron Creek watershed comprises 469,825 acres in five counties. The approximately 14,250 residents of the watershed live in rural areas or in about 30 small towns.

Major land uses are grassland (48 percent), forest land (43 percent) and crop land (0.5 percent). The topography ranges from flat flood plains to mountain elevations between 250 and 1,800 feet. The rocks in the watershed are of the Pennsylvania Atoka formation, laid down about 300 million years ago, and consisting primarily of sandstone and shale.

Cadron Creek
Geography

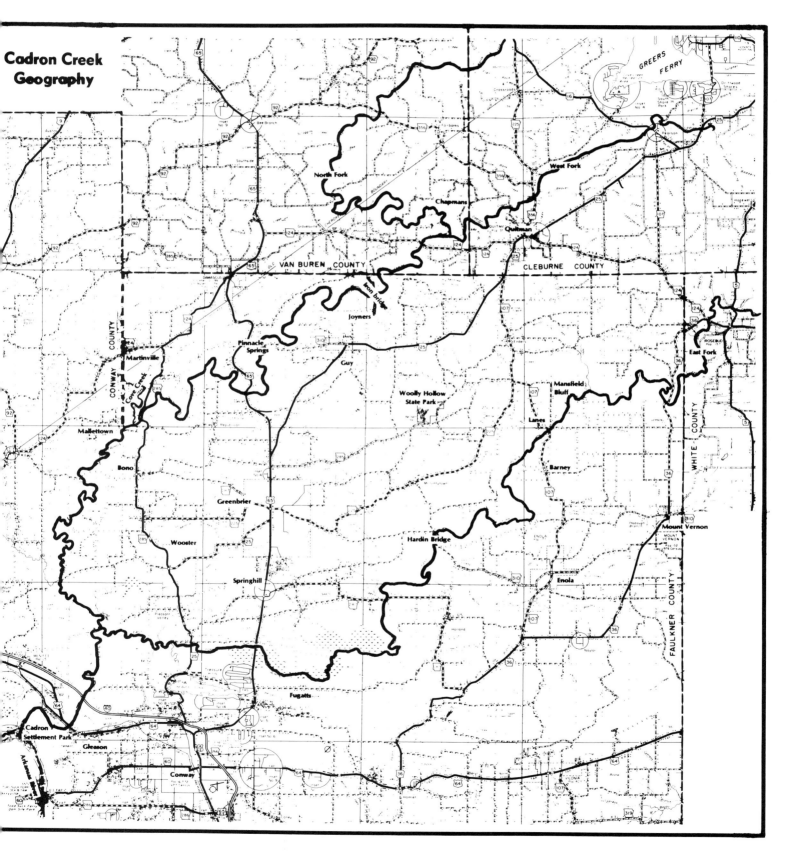

THE NORTH FORK

As forceful as a mountain stream, as sluggish as an eerie bayou, as quiet as a valley lake—the NORTH FORK of Cadron Creek has many faces throughout the year.

Users of the North Fork meet such diversities as a heron dipping toward patches of lily pads, a family of mallards gliding upstream, or heavy braided ropes hanging from tall oak trees over swimming holes. Trotlines bobbing along the edge mark favorite fishing spots. Characteristic of the North Fork are jagged pinnacles, moss-carpeted bluffs, hidden caves and large, flat rocks on its banks. Violets, columbines, fire pinks and lobelia add color along the way. Many forms of vegetation provide a habitat for kingfishers, mockingbirds, squirrel and raccoons. River birches, sycamores, gums and hickories form attractive canopies over narrow channels. As a canoeing stream, the North Fork is an inviting, pleasant creek with plenty of swift rapids, surprising curves and placid pools.

Near the Headwaters

J. Clifton Chapman

As a boy, J. Clifton Chapman loved to climb grape vines, hide in the wild azaleas and plunge into a swimming hole from a bent birch limb. Having a creek nearby gave Chapman and his pals plenty to do when they finished their farm chores. Many afternoons at the creek were spent skipping rocks across the water's surface or hunting for frogs on the banks.

"I stayed on the Cadron when I was growing up," said the husky, blue-eyed Chapman, now nearing his 71st year. "There were lots of large families through here. They'd have five or six boys and we'd spent all day long by the creek Sundays fishing, swimming, swinging from vines, wandering around. We'd just go down and play."

The North Fork of Cadron Creek borders land that has been in the Chapman family for four generations. Big Branch, a tributary, runs through the farm.

Since mill work was a large part of the area's economy, Chapman grew up hearing much about the operation. The first mill made fellys, the pieces that went around the spokes of wagon wheels. "What they did there was cut pieces of wood into different lengths—just rough cuts," he said.

Chapman was just a little boy when the felly mill operated; he remembers more about the stave bolt mill that replaced it. Many times he watched men hauling trees by horse-drawn wagons to the mill, but he was too young to go into the woods to watch the trees being felled. "We always knew when they was cutting down trees 'cause we could hear them chopping," Chapman recalled. At the mill, lumber was cut in 36-inch-long pieces, then split into quarters called stave bolts. These bolts were stripped to various widths.

"They only cut raw strips," Chapman said. "From here, they were sent to somewhere else where notches and fittings were cut and smoothed, then bent to fit barrels and nail kegs like the one in my shed. White oak was what they used. All these fields was covered with white oak," which evidently explains how White Oak Mountain, south of his farm, got its name.

After the logs were hauled to the mill, a major part of the job was grading the stave bolts. Those with knots were discarded because pieces cut for staves had to be straight. In this section of the country, years ago, people used barrels made of staves to roast hogs. "They used wooden barrels 'cause they held the heat best. They put heated rocks on the bottom. Hung hogs from a rod at the top," Chapman added.

Because these mills were powered by steam boilers, it was essential that they be near a creek. Chapman explained: "Back then, they didn't know what gas was. They had to borrow steam engines.

When they brought that ol' boiler in, why, it looked like something awful. They was pulling it with a double team of horses on the wagon from Heber Springs. But I was just a kid and it looked like a monster—that thing up in the wagon."

The raised concrete slab where the boiler sat marks the spot where stacks of timber were cut in the early part of this century. Grass and bushes now cover the area, but the narrow clear creek is the same. The old mill place was like the general store in a small town. Men "just hung around, shooting craps, or doing nothing."

Chapman was a teenager when a saw mill was opened at the old mill site. "They just added a carriage, run on a track like a train track. A man would pull a large handle to cut a long piece off the log which was on this carriage. Then he'd push that handle back and pull again to cut another piece any size they wanted. Everything was done by hand. That man would be there all day working that handle. First, they had to make the log square by cutting the bark off with four cuts."

The smell of freshly cut wood seemed to hover over the open pasture as Chapman described the screeching of the saws slicing the logs. "The old sawdust pile stayed down there a long while. I played in it a lot of times."

J. Clifton and Mavis (Trawick) Chapman live on the old home site of his ancestors in the Central community in Van Buren County, just across the Cleburne County line northwest of Quitman. Clifton's great-grandfather, William Nelson Chapman, settled there in 1820. Mavis' ancestors also lived for a while on the same land—a stone's throw from the Cadron and within earshot of the old mill place.

The Chapmans raise about 200 head of beef cattle on 455 acres. From their pink wood-frame home atop a knoll, they enjoy a landscape of open, rolling hills, spotted with woods—a reminder of the timberland where they were raised. They spend warm evenings on their front porch and cold nights around a wood-burning stove in their simply decorated living room.

Their enclosed back porch is partly filled with the harvest from their vegetable garden: sweet potatoes, onions, squash, peanuts. A huge hornet's nest, found years ago on the Cadron, hangs on the wall. The Chapmans relish the privacy of living miles from a paved road. When the gravel roads are sometimes impassable in winter, they shrug at the temporary inconvenience.

The landscape along the Cadron has changed considerably during the years that Clifton Chapman has lived in the Central community. As he talked about the past, he pointed to spots on his open grazing land: "There used to be a school down there. Fifty kids went to it. Everybody walked. There was another one two or three miles over yonder with as many kids. There used to be all houses and timber through here." A home was built wherever there was a spring, and there are plenty of springs in this northernmost watershed of the Cadron.

Today, beef cattle roam this land where cotton and corn were once row cropped. With an air of security, Chapman says that if heavy rains cause the Cadron to spill over, it just goes into pasture land. He has lost only one crop of corn in 40 years of farming—when Hurricane Betsy screamed through the area in the mid-1960's.

Walking along the edge of a fescue pasture near the creek, Chapman reminisced about the Cadron. He remembers well when he and two buddies carried a 14-foot flat bottom boat down the middle of the North Fork to fish. "It was all rock, so we'd carry the boat down to the holes and fish. Then after a while, we'd have to pick it up and move it again to another hole. My hands got sore 'cause I was holding up the back." The old holes are still favorite fishing spots for farmers who sink their hooks from johnboats and wading tubes.

Another story involved the mysterious disappearance of $600 in gold that one of the Burroughs boys kept in an eel skin. Years ago, since there were no banks nearby, people kept their money hidden in their homes. "This boy hid this eel skin with that gold in a bluff on the Cadron," recalled Chapman. "When he went down to get it, he couldn't find it. No one ever knew what became of it."

The Burroughs were close neighbors of the Chapmans and Trawicks. As we bounced over a pasture in a pickup truck one afternoon, we passed large rocks scattered around an old dug well near where the Burroughs' home once stood. Their family cemetery is hidden by trees and bushes in the middle of a pasture on the Chapman farm. This is close to Big

Mavis and J. Clifton Chapman with Benji

Branch which Chapman said has never been dry as far back as he can remember because of the deep springs.

He recalled how clear the water always was: "When I was a kid my grandfather growed oats and stuff like that and they planted rows by hand. I was the water boy, and I'd have to go out there and sink a jug in that creek and hold my hand over it until I got it to the bottom—then let it fill up. You could get as clear a water as out of a well." The creek is still clear and cool.

Even stories of historical note have been passed down through the generations—stories of the Yankee soldiers who walked along the creek after capturing Little Rock during the Civil War, of Jesse James who hid his horses in the Cadron's bluffs between Quitman and Bee Branch and a few times visited the Burroughs' home.

The Chapmans live only a few miles from where the West Fork of the Cadron meets the North Fork, about one-half mile north of Highway 124. "From the forks to where it headed was 10 miles across the fill and 40 miles around it. That's what my grandfather always said. He was just guessing, but that's close," Chapman said.

A high bluff, resembling an open-faced cave, forms a rounded wall at a 90-degree bend in the West Fork. On this bend is Round Hole, once a popular social spot where young couples partied and were serenaded by screech owls. Today, kids still try to out-jump each other from the braided rope tied from a high limb over the water. Baptist and Methodist

Along West Fork

church-goers know Round Hole as the place for baptisms; some still are performed there occasionally.

It's about a half-hour walk along a thickly wooded bank from Round Hole to the confluence of the North and West Forks. Except for the little-used private farm road to Round Hole, there is no road access to the junction. Huge oaks, some measuring three feet in diameter, are living signs that this area was unscathed by the teeth of saws that cleared most of the virgin timber in these Ozark foothills years ago. The woods are as dense, right up to the water's edge, as a jungle.

Both forks sneak to the merging point through narrow channels, darkened by arched trees and steep, brush-covered banks. The North Fork makes a sharp right turn to join the West Fork coming straight ahead. The creek then widens and begins to drop into a rhythm of easy ripples and long pools. From this junction on, the creek is labeled on some maps as Cadron Creek and on others as the North Cadron.

The Chapmans are so proud of the Cadron Creek that borders their farm that they refer to it as "our Cadron Creek." Although the pioneers' landscape of homes and barns sheltered by oak groves has changed to one of open pastures and scattered patches of trees, the swimming holes they splashed in are still there, and the blood roots, poke and chinquapins they knew still grow on the banks. The paths they ran along through the brush and briars have been kept worn by others who have known the peace of rural life growing up along the Cadron.

The Iron Bridge (Old Hartwick Mill Place)

As you descend the steep, curved gravel road from North Guy, a view of hills, pastures and fence posts seems to extend to infinity. Tucked in a bed of trees, the concealed Cadron might be miles away. But as the road straightens at the bottom of the hill, the creek begins to reveal itself. A high truss bridge, with heavy planks that rattle as vehicles cross, peeks through the river birches like a rusted skeleton. Tire tracks in the worn roadways and weedy fields and stone-enclosed circles of charred wood tell that others have been here before. Canoeists refer to this spot on the Cadron as the "iron bridge," but old-timers still call it the "mill bridge" or the "old Hartwick mill place."

"Uncle" Tubby Hartwick settled near this area in northern Faulkner County in 1830 and built a grist mill and wooden dam here in 1868. Ownership passed on to his son Jake and his grandson Dick. About the turn of the century, Jim Bean of Guy bought the mill. He sold it about 1910 to John Mode, who replaced the wooden dam with a rock one in 1911. The following year the iron bridge was constructed, eliminating the often hazardous fording of the creek by mule-drawn wagons which brought corn and wheat from farms north of the creek to be ground at the mill. The old mill, largest in the area, was washed away in 1927, ending an era of prosperous economy for the community. Stacked rocks from the old dam remain on both sides of the creek.

Just as farmers today keep the benches warm in front of the Guy grocery stores, their ancestors gathered at the Hartwick mill to discuss the weather, crops and politics. Both young and old also swam, fished and picnicked here. "Just about everybody showed up Sunday nights when there was baptizing," said one farmer who witnessed many of these ceremonies, "and we'd bring a basket of food and lunch up on the bank."

People still gather at the iron bridge to swim and fish, crowding its open banks on hot summer weekends and holidays. Over the years it has become a popular put in spot for canoeists floating to Pinnacle Springs and a camping site for those floating from the upper stretches.

The road crossing the creek here, once the Clinton to Little Rock road, still is a well-traveled link for Van Buren County residents heading south to the major highways.

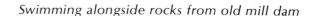

Swimming alongside rocks from old mill dam

One Who Remembers

"As a kid, on Sundays we played around the mill area. I walked on top of that bridge many a time. Climbed all over the bluffs." Octogenarian Albert Presley, who spent part of his younger life in Guy, was referring to the old Hartwick mill place. When not splashing in the Cadron or fishing for perch from a rock on the edge, Presley was unloading corn from his family's wagon at the mill. He forded the creek many times before the bridge was built in 1912: "If we didn't have some good, sturdy mules, it would have been real hard crossing."

A cave in the hill south of the creek was a favorite place for kids to explore. "We used to go down in that cave," remembers Presley. "During the war, Hartwick kept meat in there to keep the Jayhawks from getting it. It was a narrow crevice in the rock. They harrowed out a place to keep food."

Albert Presley

As a young man, Presley experienced many of the problems that farmers faced on their trips to Conway where they sold some of their grain and bought merchandise. On one of these trips, Presley and his brother Doug drove their wagons through Linder and over the old Terry Bridge on the East Cadron to buy fertilizer. (The original Terry Bridge was on a farm road south of where it now crosses the Cadron on Highway 287.)

"We came upon a big rain on the way back the next day," said Presley. "Water came up to the floor of the wagons. We got past the bridge with water sloshing up inside. Then one of the wagons dumped in a chuck hole and broke a coupling pole. We had to hook one wagon to the other, hitched both teams of mules in front to get home about 10 that night—with no lights. Had to keep on. We knew the water was a-moving."

The tall, bespectacled Presley looks more like a professional businessman than a former farmer. Suits showing years of wear have replaced the overalls and denim shirts of his earlier days. His face lacks the weathered lines and ruddiness of a life spent outdoors. He speaks decisively and discreetly.

Presley has done as much as anyone to keep the memory of the old Hartwick mill alive. His sketch of the mill was printed in the Sunday magazine of the *Arkansas Gazette* in October 1937, accompanying a story about a wood block of the mill carved by Mrs. Vivian Utley. A painting (on a piece of corrugated cardboard) of the mill and bridge site hangs with several other paintings on his living room wall. "I did it just from my memory," he said humbly.

The creative talents of Presley go beyond his paintings and sketches. He made a fiddle years ago and "played it like a master," according to one of his long-time friends. He also wrote poetry. "I'd just come in sometime and write. No special reason." The subjects of his poems vary from nature to people to places, many based on Biblical references.

Presley speaks shyly about his talents. He's lost the interest he once had in painting and writing but not in the stories and memory of the Hartwick mill place and the Cadron.

One poem he proudly shows to visitors is pasted to the back of the painting of the mill, alongside a yellowing piece of paper listing names and dates associated with the mill:

Old Hartwick mill site at iron bridge

The Old Mill

Down under the hill,
There stands an old mill,
On the banks of a beautiful stream.
In its brown-coated dress,
I long have caressed,
As an ideal of my dreams.

Down under the hill,
By the old mill,
In the shade of the oak and the birch,
I gaily took up my line and hook
and fished for the dainty perch.

Down under the hill,
Stands the old mill,
As a token of days of old.
When I used to play
To the water spray
of my boyhood swimming hole.

                    ALP

Painting of old mill site by Albert Presley

Near site of old government whiskey still between iron bridge and Pinnacle Springs

A Community United by the Creek

When people from the farming community of Guy in northern Faulkner County get together to reminisce, stories about Cadron Creek abound.

"Oh, we played up and down that creek," said Venice Joyner, a petite woman in her early sixties. "Always a-doin' something."

When her daughter was young, Mrs. Joyner would take her and her friends to the bluff for Sunday afternoon picnics. "There's a cave down there and some of the boys would think they was brave and go in a-ways. They never knew what was in there, but they'd have tales about snakes and things." It's been years since Venice Joyner was on the bluff, but she was there so often in her youth that the memory is vivid. "If I go straight from out of the house here, I could find it. At the end of this pasture."

Venice and her husband Darse were neighbors while growing up. He "lived on the corner where the road turns to go down hill to the creek." She lived "up the road a bit near the schoolhouse." For the past 40 years, the Joyners have lived in an old wood frame home with an open porch across the front. The windows are covered with plastic on the outside to keep out the wind and dust. Only a pasture separates them from the creek.

For several years, Darse worked in Little Rock (about a 60-mile drive) to supplement the income from their small farm. First, they raised dairy cows, then beef cattle. Now they raise rabbits. In their large garden, surrounded by boysenberry bushes and peach trees, they grow enough corn, squash, potatoes, okra and tomatoes to last through the winter.

Robert Mode, whose family farmed adjacent to the Joyners, was a boyhood buddy of Darse. Mode's Uncle John Mode owned the old Hartwick mill on the Cadron in the early part of the century when Joyner's father worked there.

As children, Mode and Joyner often hung around the mill place, peering into the rugged wooden

Darse and Venice Joyner

building set out over the water, watching the huge, round stones rub against each other as they crushed corn and wheat and spit the meal into wooden containers. Their laughter was muted by the splashing of water as the large wheel turned and by the whooshing of grains as they spilled into the hopper. They climbed the crossbars of the iron bridge, calling to farmers as their wagons, heaped with grain, clattered over the wooden planks. Sometimes they jumped onto wagons, hitching a ride up the steep hill to their homes.

"My daddy ran that mill for John Mode a good long time," Joyner said proudly. "I remember that dam they built across the creek. That water just come in there and turned that wheel. That was all the power they had. I spent many a hour down there."

While he rolled a pinch of tobacco into a cigarette, Joyner described how the wheel worked: "There was a gate where the water went in and a big old slab up higher which they'd pull down to cut the water off and stop the wheel. When they got ready to run those stones, they'd wind the thing up and that water'd start again. When it hit that big wheel, the mill went."

The size of the water wheel and of the grinding stones seemed massive to the wide-eyed youngsters. The old-timers talk with enthusiasm about the mill's operation. "They had wheat rocks and corn rocks. Those were **large** rocks. This ground wheat made what we called graham bread," explained Joyner. "Had no way of bleaching it, you know. It was just brown bread, brown flour. Why, they'd come from miles and miles—from Bee Branch, some of them—to get corn ground there. By wagon loads, lined up the road. That wheel turned all day."

The Hartwick mill was one of the largest grist mills on the Cadron. Farmers came not only to get grains ground but also to hear the latest news, fish, or just "chew the fat." Sometimes there were so many wagons along the road that farmers had to wait for days before they could get their grains ground. "My daddy would fill his big wagon with grains from several families and just camp there until it all got ground," said Mode in his musing voice.

While we sat around the Joyners' kitchen table, enjoying homemade pumpkin pie and iced tea, stories about past years on the Cadron continued. "I remember hearing my daddy and all the neighbors tellin' that when it rained, they'd bring wheat and corn and have to wait a long time to have it ground," said Venice Joyner. "They'd all sit down there and catch fish while they was a-waitin'. The fish would come to eat from the wheat and corn that would fall from the mill. They'd catch lots of fish. My daddy would come home with a pail of fish many a-time."

Darse added: "When the water was up, that concrete enclosed an area as big as this room, and fish would come in there. You'd get a mess of 'em. That's when you caught fish!"

Downstream from the mill, a fish trap once lay across the Cadron. "There's kind of a V-shape in the creek there," Mode recalled. "That was the fish trap. When water would get up, then fish would come down the creek and couldn't get back. They'd just lay up there by the trap and people would get all the fish they wanted."

Still further downstream was a bluff where kids fished from some 30 feet up. "We'd pull them all the way up the side of that bluff," Mode continued. "You could just sit there and watch them in the water."

Listening to these reminiscences, you can almost hear the sizzling from the skillets frying a batch of fish for supper back in the kitchen. One imagines overall-clad youngsters heading up the dusty road with a string of fish dangling from tree branch poles extending beyond their lean shoulders. Served with the fresh water fish was freshly-baked corn bread, a staple food on the table of every home.

"Now, that corn bread was not like the corn bread you eat today. It was altogether different bread—and it was good!" said Joyner, his eyebrows rising. "It was coarse, you know. Didn't get hot. Was ground on big rocks, **large** rocks. It was slower ground and, oh, it was **delicious** bread!"

Mrs. Joyner added that "you don't have to sift the

Old mill place below iron bridge

Wood used in Mode's home came from one of the hotels at Pinnacle Springs

Robert Mode

meal you buy now in a paper sack, unless you want to, but you really had to sift that meal and then you had a lot of bran left through and you sifted that."

Fishing and hanging around the old mill place were not the only pastimes of the children. They roamed miles of the creek's banks, climbing high trees and crevices in the bluffs, jumping rocks across low levels in the water, or just sprawling among the chionanthus and farkleberry bushes in the shades of the sycamores and oaks. In the heat of the summer, the youngsters found seclusion in the wooded areas beyond the creek, their shrill voices accented by the drilling of the pileated woodpeckers on tree trunks.

"On Thanksgiving once, a group of us boys went

swimming in the creek," Mode remembered. "Pretty cold then, I tell ya. We also hunted on both sides. Why, we'd just pull our shoes off and wade across. It was terrible to step in there, so cold, but our feet stayed warm when we put our shoes on. After we chased a few rabbits, we'd come back the same way."

Squirrels, 'coons and 'possums also were hunted around the bluffs on the Cadron.

"I was comin' up that bluff (below his home) a-hunting at night when you had to crawl," Darse Joyner said, edging to the front of his chair. "There's a place under that bluff, if you fall off, it would be about 100 feet you'd fall. I'd been up there many a night—at midnight—with the dogs huntin' and just on my

hands and knees crawlin'. If you had one little slip, that was all of it and you knowed it. But I wasn't scared. It didn't bother me. I enjoyed huntin' down there." Joyner isn't sure now where he'd come in under that bluff, but "back then, I could find it blind-folded," he boasted.

J. D. Pratt sat in an old stuffed armchair in the Joyner home one cold winter day, discussing with Joyner and Mode the rabbits they chased from bushes and the strings of fish they caught in the Cadron. Pratt now lives in Conway but returns often to visit his friends and rehash favorite tales: "There ain't a rock on those bluffs I haven't overturned. We was down there whenever we got our chores done."

Along with the sweet fragrance of wildflowers and plants that have always brightened the Cadron route was the damp, sour odor of the whiskey stills which in pre-Prohibition days played a part in the life of the Guy community. One government-owned still was about midway from the iron bridge to Pinnacle Springs, near one of the flattop bluffs frequently used as a lunch stop by canoeists. Stillhouse Creek, which enters the Cadron a few feet above the iron bridge, was named for a privately-run whiskey still just across the road from Joyner's boyhood home. A spring near where the still operated remains active. "It's just over that fence where this road comes to a "T" (on the way to the Cadron). There's a big hole of water there as big as a room," said Mode. "That spring never goes dry."

Joyner and Mode were too young to go to the stills, but they heard enough about them to know that many jugs rode out of the woods in the back of the wagons. "I knowed of farmers who would take their corn down there, just shell it, then make the mash and sour that stuff to make whiskey out of it," said Mode. "I reckon after seeing how that stuff was made was why my daddy never did drink."

A "vacation" for these youngsters was a trip to Conway, about 25 miles south, to sell some of the harvest and to buy merchandise. "We'd leave early in the morning and get there around three in the after-noon—by wagon. We'd sell our cotton, buy our goods, stay in a wagon yard. Cooked in that yard a lot of times," recalled Joyner. "They'd have boarding houses down there. You could get in for 35 cents. And they'd bring up biscuits by the wash tub full. These folks, these old farmers, could eat, I tell you. **Thirty-five cents**!" he added, shaking his head.

Those who now canoe the North Cadron from the iron bridge downstream see nothing of the mill activity, of boys jumping the bluffs or climbing the trees, of grain-filled wagons wobbling down the roads, of the simple structures at the whiskey still sites. We can only imagine what it was like as we pass lichen-tinged rocks, water trickling from fissures in

the bluffs, clumps of perennial flora on the sandy banks imprinted with small animal tracks, tiny streams slipping into the creek, low-sailing hawks and sap-sucking woodpeckers.

Although the Cadron once was a lifeline in the local economy, today it is used mainly for pleasure and recreation. A Spanish philosopher, Juan Ortega y Gasset, once wrote: "I am I plus my circumstances." The Joyners and Modes, like most of their generation who grew up on the Cadron near Guy, support this philosophy. "We can't get away. We might not have a domino hall when we got anywhere else," said Darse Joyner, one of the regulars at the domino table in the back room of the Guy Grocery.

"These are my friends here. These are my people. They're here. My friends. When you get to my age, it's hard to get away. I just wouldn't be satisfied. Well, I'd just go all to pieces. If you moved me off to Conway or Little Rock or somewhere—a different environment—I couldn't take it," Joyner sighed as he sat back in his chair. "We don't have fancy rugs and nice painted walls, but this is how we are, just ordinary people, and we want it that way." Sitting on a couch lined with handmade cushions, Venice Joyner smiled and nodded: "We've been here 40 years in this house and we're happy here."

A strong commitment toward each other and toward a hard but simple life is most important to these people. They are united through respect and concern for one another—a unity born during their childhood days together along the Cadron. They speak from their hearts; they are products of their rural environment—and they like it.

"Sometimes a wagon full of kids would come to swim until sundown."

Swimming and picnicking are summer fun on the east bank at Pinnacle Springs, west of Guy.

Pinnacle Springs

In the late 1880's, the community of Pinnacle Springs flourished high on the west bank of the North Cadron between Damascus and Guy. People in search of a spa traveled there from throughout the state. At that time, 13 springs of different waters existed within a square mile near the community. The springs possessed a rare combination of gases and minerals which were said to give the water unusual curative and stimulative

George Glover

properties. High percentages of carbonate of iron and manganese were found in the water as well as glairine, a substance very rare in springs of this kind.

During its heyday of the 1880's, Pinnacle Springs had 12 bath houses, two large hotels, eight stores, a skating rink, a cotton gin, a post office, a newspaper, a college and some 50 homes scattered on the ridges. The largest hotel was called Pinnacle House, a two-story hotel of 40 rooms owned by Capt. W. W. Martin and his brother J. D. Martin.

A story in the August 3, 1889, issue of the *Log Cabin Democrat* in Conway noted: "Pinnacle Springs is remarkable for healthfulness and natural beauty. It was selected as the site for the Arkansas Christian College because of its central location and its wonderful sanitary advantages. Its altitude is such as to preclude malarial influence and prevent the debilitating effects resulting from heat in places less favorably situated."

Only two years later, however, the post office closed and the community began to wane. Some of the buildings were moved to Cadron Cove (now Martinville). In time, trees and underbrush covered much of the land that once was Pinnacle Springs community, leaving no trace of its prosperity.

Although the community has been defunct for almost 90 years, stories of its fate linger. George Glover of Guy, born shortly after the turn of the century, says that he heard that Jesse James stayed at one of the hotels. "Hid out there. That's why people stopped coming."

Another speculation on the demise of the community is the absence of a bridge spanning the Cadron at Pinnacle Springs. Historian Robert L. Gatewood, in *Faulkner County Arkansas 1778-1964*, wrote that crossing the Cadron was not dependable, especially in high water. Yet, old-timers speak of several fords upstream that were regular wagon routes across the Cadron.

The *Biographical History 1886* records that "Pinnacle Springs is free from saloons, theatres and other places so alluring to perniciousness," but Gatewood lists a saloon among the buildings in the community. Several Guy residents verify the latter reference. Glover remembers as a child a saloon that stood on the east side of the creek where people now picnic, swim and fish. Perhaps the saloon, being across the Cadron from the community, was not considered by some as part of Pinnacle Springs.

Pinnacle Springs community was named for the many springs in the area and for the two pinnacles towering to some 160 feet about

Atop west pinnacle

one-half mile downstream. The pinnacles appear to be remnants of a mountain through which the rushing Cadron cut a path. The west pinnacle is the more splendid. From the creek, the spire looks unscalable, yet it can be climbed from the south side easily or from the steep creekside by the more daring. From the top, where the rocks flatten and extend into a pasture behind, a landscape of valleys and hills rolls into the distance, with shining glimpses of the Cadron winding miles away.

The east pinnacle resembles most bluffs on the creek, a high wall of irregular sandstone, spotted with saxifrages and colored lichens. Behind is the Hidden Beauty, a lofty peak which appears to be divided into two pinnacles. Hidden Beauty is so named because it cannot be seen from creek level.

Beyond this area, called Pinnacle Gap, the Cadron zigzags its way among mountain steeps and crags into a wooded valley and through a series of pools named by owners of the bath houses at Pinnacle Springs. These pools were some of the original 13 springs. Bobbing plastic containers mark the trot lines of fishermen along the edges of Professor's Pool, Spring Lake and Grotto Bathing Pool. Aged, twisted ropes still hang from tree limbs over still popular swimming holes.

Rock formations along this stretch also were named years ago. Owl's Home, a high, broad bluff where a horned owl's nest still perches, stands like a dead-end wall beyond Professor's Pool which fades into a wide bend of ripples.

Just at the foot of Owl's Home is a side channel veering to the left, moving slowly over logs and stones, alongside tall cane, and around the base of the bluff, joining the main current about a half mile downstream. Walkers along this channel see many mussel shells, 'coon tracks, drift-wood and wake robin flowers. In times of high water, the channel is floatable.

A long pool, with Blow Out Bluff along its west side, turns into the most challenging set of rapids on this stretch of the creek. At the beginning of the rapids, a channel to the right goes around Turkey Island.

Beyond Spring Lake is Bear's Cave, a rounded cavity in a bluff on the left bank, about 50 feet from the creek. Water trickles from several layers of overhangs. In the winter, huge icicles encase the cave-like formation in jeweled majesty.

To historians, Pinnacle Springs was a community with a reputation as a thriving summer and health resort. To canoeists, Pinnacle Springs is a popular put in and take out spot on the east bank of the Cadron. To local residents, this area is a retreat for swimming, fishing, picnicking and camping. On any hot weekend, the east bank (across from where the community once existed) is crowded with people and pickups.

A Lifetime of Fishing and Hunting

"I lived my whole life on that 'Nord' Cadron. Hunted it. Fished it. Was on it day and night and still go down there." The North Cadron has been as much a part of Derwayne Battles' life as baling hay and plowing his fields. He knows the creek as well as the contours of his land.

"I've been in that Cadron from one end to the 'utter.' Where it meets the East Fork to where it starts up there above Quitman. I could tell you anything about any place on that creek," Battles boasted as he named Jim Ford, Suck Ford, Big Rock Hole, Twin Holes and other spots. He described Twin Holes as "two little holes of water that look alike. Just a little shoals between them."

"That ol' Cadron doesn't look nothing like it did. There used to be fords all along there for wagons to cross," Battles said. "You could never tell there was roads there now. All along that Cadron you can find rocks like this sidewalk and as big. They're not roads—just pieces of the bluff that fell off."

The 64-year-old Battles said he had the happiest time of his life on the creek. "Was somewhere on that 'Nord' Cadron every weekend. If I could start over, I don't think I'd relive my life any different. I had a lot of fun like it was."

Battles lives on his family's old homestead west of Guy. His land extends to the Cadron a short distance upstream from Pinnacle Springs. Crowds still gather at the swimming holes but not like they did in Battles' younger years when people spent more time near home.

"I've seen as high as 500 people there at Pinnacle Springs. That's where everyone used to go for the

Derwayne Battles

whole weekend," drawled Battles. "I've seen people have to wait for people to come out of the water. That's how many there used to be. They came with wagons and teams and tied them in the fields top a that hill (above the creek). For a quarter mile on both banks they'd be as thick as they could stand. On Sunday after church, everybody went to the creek. The whole community went there together. We visited that way. This was a religious community. Everybody helped out the sick and the 'widdered' women. We'd all go to cut wood, help in the garden. Work all day, then have a singin' at night. Have an old-timey square dance. Sprinkled a litle cornmeal on the floor and danced all night. We neighbored that way."

A chain saw accident 12 years ago left Battles with a limp foot. This has slowed him down a little but not enough to keep him from farming, helping with the senior citizens' program, cleaning at the school—and spending time on the Cadron: "I still fish as much as I did. I get a kick at getting that first one. Pulled out a bass that weighed 9¼ pounds. It measured from the tip of this big finger to my ribs," he said, stretching out his arm.

"The best tastin' fish you can get" is how Battles describes catches from the Cadron. "Any fish taken out of this Cadron is a good eatin' fish 'cause it's a cool, clear stream of water—a rock bottom creek, most of it. You just take your pole when you float this Cadron and you'll get fish. I guarantee it."

Battles also still enjoys hunting, even though his walking is hampered by his injured foot. His sharp eye is acknowledged by his neighbors. "He can shoot a kernal of corn out of your hand. The best shot around here," was the praise from one of his friends. Battles smiled shyly, saying, "I'd take him along to carry the pelts. I still got a pack of dogs and 'coon hunt along that 'Nord' Cadron. Good huntin' there."

As long as the North Cadron continues to flow past Derwayne Battles' farm, he'll be there casting his line or sighting his gun. "I believe that everybody's got a time to go. We don't know when that time is. But I know that I'll be on that Cadron until my time comes."

The Final Stretch

Six college students lugged their colorful fiberglass canoes up the steep path from the Cadron under the Highway 65 bridge. Jeans dripping wet, feet squishing in soiled sneakers, their first float from Pinnacle Springs had been fun, and they talked of returning the next weekend. The Highway 65 bridge is a popular put in and take out spot for canoeists.

The terrain on the long stretch from Highway 65 to Highway 285 changes frequently and abruptly from bluff-lined hills of some 200 feet to wooded areas at creek level. In places, the Cadron tumbles like a mountain stream, concealed by high, rocky banks and leaning trees. In other places, the creek widens to accommodate several willow-clad sand islands and a choice of navigable channels. The swift turns and narrow shoots alongside cliff walls make this float trip one of the most challenging on the North Cadron. About five miles downstream is the infamous "Rock of Gibraltar." Rising about 20 feet above water like a glacier, the mighty rock has dented and capsized many a canoe drawn into it by the strong current.

Most characteristic of this part of the North Cadron are the bluffs. Long and towering, jagged and smooth, they alternate from one side of the creek to the other on this ribbon-like route. One picturesque

Floating safely around the "Rock of Gilbraltar."

formation is Alum Bluff, the first large bluff on the right bank. Behind the white splotched rocks is Alum Cave, one of the most intriguing natural features on the Cadron. Years ago people walked to this bluff and cave to obtain alum which they used to stop bleeding, to make pickles and to use as a mordant in natural dyeing.

Illusion Bluff, about one mile from Highway 285, is a spectacular sight. Because its layers of rock lie at an angle to the creek, canoeists have the illusion of paddling uphill alongside the long, pink and yellow tinted formation. Illusion Bluff was a big attraction for young people in the early part of this century. They came from miles around to swim and picnic. "We'd have to climb that big bluff to get to a rope that we'd swing from high in the trees over the water," recalled Victor Halter who rode to the area from Conway many times. "There were lots of big trees that went out over the creek. We had fun up there."

On the hill above Illusion Bluff are the remains of an old rock cabin built in the early 1920's by the Pack and Grid Hiking Association from Hendrix College in Conway. Elizabeth "Tip" Reynolds Davidson, Bryant Davidson and Dr. Henry Wilbur Camp organized the Pack and Grid group in 1922 at a meeting in the home of Dr. John H. Reynolds, Hendrix president and Tip's father. To join the club one had to hike 20 miles in a day.

"There was a group of us who hiked all around that area looking for a site to build a cabin, said Tip Davidson who was a freshman when the association was started. "I remember once in January, Bryant (who later became her husband) and I were fording Cove Creek on one of these trips and we got in over our waists so we decided to just swim across. Then we went home in an open touring car and it was as cold as it could be. But we were in good shape and never took a cold. In the summer that creek was hardly knee deep.

"We did all the rock work on the cabin ourselves, even the fireplace. We were a pretty rough crowd and all of us could handle an ax," said Tip, who served as chairman of the building committee. "Got a truck and just went through the woods getting rock together. A carpenter did the wood part. I took the man out every morning before classes and went to get him in the afternoon. I about flunked out that semester because I was up there so much." No road led to the cabin site when construction began, but they made so many trips that the route they traveled looked like a road. Since the cabin wasn't completed until the fall of 1925, Tip's senior year at Hendrix, she didn't get much time to use it (she graduated in January). But during its construction, she and her group camped and hiked almost every weekend in the Cove Creek area and farther.

"We did an amazing amount of hiking," said Mrs. Davidson. "We'd just stop somewhere and sleep out. We didn't have tents—oh, maybe once in a while we did, but we just had knapsacks and army blankets—no sleeping bags." Hiking 40 or more miles a day was nothing to these students in those days, she said. "We had to have a chaperone on all our trips. Dr. Camp

was usually with us anyway and sometimes Dr. Robert Campbell (both were Hendrix professors). "But when we went on overnight trips, we had to have a woman chaperone. My older sister (Ruth Reynolds Driver) often went along or Ethel Miller."

The Pack and Grid group did some boating on both Cadron and Cove Creeks, using flat bottom boats since they didn't have canoes then. "One time we took a trip in a flat bottom and the water was so swift. I was in the stern and would have turned the boat over if I hadn't caught on a limb. I let the boat go ahead and I lost my pants," laughed Mrs. Davidson. "We did a lot of frog gigging with lanterns on our foreheads right there below the cabin. But I wasn't on that creek too much. We did more hiking all over that area from the Cadron to Cove Creek." According to a local resident, the Pack and Grid cabin was ransacked and burned in the 1930's.

Some 30 years ago, Ely Sam of Martinville used to walk this stretch of the Cadron fishing. Parents driving children from his hometown to the Greenbrier school would leave Sam at the Highway 65 bridge, then pick him up on their way home from school in

Illusion Bluff

the afternoon on Highway 285, about 11 miles downstream.

Mr. and Mrs. Cotton Reynolds of the Republican community occasionally drive through their pastures and wooded areas to fish in the Cadron. "It's just a narrow road and steep, but you can make your way around the bluff in a four-wheel drive," said Mrs. Reynolds. She also knows about the rock that canoeists call "Gibraltar." "That's right out from here," she said, pointing in the direction of the road they take to go fishing. "A lot of 'em don't make it past that."

As we stood on a huge moss-covered boulder projecting from the side of the steep incline above the bluffs, we could hear the rushing Cadron. When the wind swayed the trees, we could see the creek— far below.

The terrain along the Cadron drops drastically in elevation a few hundred feet downstream where David Reynolds and his family have a picnic table under the trees near the creek below their farm. "They love to go down there. Cook hamburgers, fish. The children have fun running through there to the creek," Mrs. Reynolds said of her son's family.

Those who grew up near the Cadron on Highway 285 often mention the name "Bogaloosha" as this area once was called because it resembled a region so-named in the Louisiana bogs. Mrs. Ophelia Mallett Garrett, for whose ancestors Mallettown was named (west of the Cadron in Conway County), said that in the early part of this century there were so many saw mills and so much timber here that everyone just called it "Bogaloosha." Early maps carried the name for the area between Damascus and Bono.

"There's no creek around that's had more mills than the Cadron," said Mrs. Garrett. "When one mill went out, another came in or one would move a little farther up the creek." Saw mills run by Seth and Ed Oliver, Ruf Lucas and others were scattered along the creek and road.

Devil's Chimney on Cove Creek, a Cadron tributary just a few hundred feet from Highway 285, has been a natural attraction for years. The stepped, spire-like formation looks as if someone piled rocks on top of one another. This stretch of Cove Creek that passes Devil's Chimney is floatable from Martinville to the Cadron. To take out, however, canoeists must either continue one mile down the Cadron to the Mallet-town bridge or paddle upstream to the Highway 285 bridge.

With the exception of a few pastures, once covered with trees but cleared by the saw mill operators, the land bordering the Cadron near Highway 285 is mainly wooded, giving the creek a secluded setting.

Devil's Chimney on Cove Creek

Knowing the Cadron is being a part of the rocks, the ripples and every living thing in its environment.

Opossum

Azalias

French mulberry

58

Atop Illusion Bluff on the North Fork

Fire pink

Day-flower

Around every bend is
a new challenge, a new
discovery, a new
character.

Between the iron bridge and Pinnacle Springs on the North Fork

Raccoon

Butterfly-weed

Near junction of the West and North Forks

THE EAST FORK

The EAST FORK of Cadron Creek offers a special place to learn and love the creek environment. Conspicuous among many hardwoods, cedars and pines are a large variety of wildflowers like golden frost asters, evening primrose, wild iris, water purslane and jack-in-the-pulpits. In streamside communities are minks, otters and raccoons. Beavers build dens along the waterway rather than dams and lodges found elsewhere in the state. Cranes and herons are among the dozens of birds in the creek's environment. Schools of fish feed among twisted tree roots mirrored in the water's surface. Most characteristic of the East Fork are the contorted grotesque tupelo trees, standing like sentinels in and along the creek.

The combination of towering bluffs, picturesque waterfalls, wildlife and a variety of plants make the East Fork different and intriguing—a canoeist's delight and a fisherman's paradise. Favorite fishing spots are evident by paths that extend along the bank from one hole to another. Around every bend is a new discovery, a new challenge, a new character.

The Cadron at Their Back Door

"I've had so many children come from school. There was more times than there wasn't that my five children would come off the bus, and they'd have five more, a buddy apiece. They'd go fishing and swimming in the creek. Come back starved to death and I'd have a lot of food cooked for them on the table. I'd just back up out of the way and watch 'em eat," smiled Mrs. Myrtle Lane. It was common for the Lane home to be filled with friends. "In the winter, they'd come to skate on the creek. I've seen it froze across a lot of times, but maybe not in the middle it wouldn't be froze enough because it's deeper," she continued.

"Every summer people from way off would come up here to swim. It would take a few hours to come by wagon or foot from Enola (about seven miles south). My children would come in, get their swimsuits and run to the creek. Sometimes a wagon full of kids would come to swim until sundown."

Mrs. Lane and her son James live just off Highway 107, two miles north of Barney. Another son John lives up the road on her family's old homestead. Their 280 acres border part of the most floatable stretch of the East Fork of Cadron Creek.

The Lanes love to share the pleasures that the Cadron has provided them through the years. Their welcome is always warm to friends and visitors who stop to chat after canoeing or who come to hike the creek on their property. Seldom does anyone leave without lunch, a glass of iced tea, a cup of coffee or a piece of homemade pie.

Mrs. Lane, in her late sixties, speaks fondly of her children and grandchildren and often mentions "those nice people who were here last week to walk to the bluff." She keeps busy freezing and canning fruits and vegetables from her garden, crocheting afghans and baking breads, pies and biscuits. Her sons James and John work in Conway, some 25 miles away, since they no longer farm or raise cattle. They often join float trips using their johnboat, which doesn't take the turns as easily as a canoe. "We get a little wet, but it's all in fun," laughed James. Even when they don't float, they usually visit with canoeists at the

John, James and Myrtle Lane

creek and are reliable forecasters of the floating conditions. Knowing how to determine the best floatable water level is important on the popular stretch that passes alongside the Lane farm because it can be a tiring, canoe-dragging trip in low water and a dangerous float around the tupelo gum trees in the fast current in high water. "When the water is around these trees, it's just right," said James, pointing out two prominent tupelos on the bank at the take out place near the Highway 107 bridge. The knot below the carved letters in the one tree is a good indicator. "But, if you see the water up in these bushes (beyond the trees), don't try it."

Boys in pre-World War II days, the Lane brothers still enjoy gigging frogs and taking their boat to Cedar Branch Hole to fish. Reflecting on such memories as catching snakes to take home and trying to flip off the highest limb into the swimming hole has deepened their appreciation of the Cadron. Now, John's sons enjoy catching frogs and hopping stones in the creek as much as the older Lanes did. "They run in here, grab their fishing poles, head right for the creek,"said Mrs. Lane. "Sometimes they spend hours just playing down there."

One of the most beautiful natural phenomena on the East Cadron is Mansfield Bluff, reaching to heights of nearly 100 feet for about a half mile along the north bank between Highways 36 and 107. The almost vertical formation of sandstone and shale is smooth in places and scallopped in others. Water seeping through cracks makes the rock black. Near its east end is Rainbow Falls, jetting over a pointed ledge about 80 feet above the creek. We always stop here on float trips, each time noticing a new rock formation or a different color pattern on the wet wall.

Mansfield Bluff is a little more than a mile walk through the Lane farm—over cattle paths, across pastures, along narrow farm roads lined with cane, through cedar groves and along the Cadron. During any season, the walk is inspired by the serenity and variety of the vast environment. Mansfield Bluff supports the scene around the creek like a backdrop.

Walk to Mansfield Bluff

James Lane at Mansfield Bluff

Standing beneath it can be hypnotic. No matter where you look, startling new designs imprint your mind. On one of my winter walks to the bluff, I stood in one spot by the creek and filled two rolls of film with facets of its splendor.

Early one spring, while I marveled at the wavy ledges and fissures along the bluff wall, James Lane pointed to one crack about 50 feet up: "When I was a kid, I used to climb up there. Couldn't do that now. Of course, back then, it seemed easy."

Further down the bluff are two cave-like indentations about 30 feet above the ground. "We climbed up into those caves lots of times. It would be hard to get around that ledge now. A lot of rock has broke off. For all the times I've been up here—and that was every chance I got—I never saw any rock fall, but it looks like it's falling all the time," James said, looking at pieces scattered over the ground.

We walked closer to the creek on our way back, noting many trees felled by beavers. Most were sweet gums. James picked off a piece of the gum with his knife. It stuck to my fingers like glue. "We used to chew that," he said. "It's better if you boil it. Many people used to get a big batch and boil it to get rid of the stickiness."

A walk to Mansfield Bluff was a weekly outing for the Lane family when the children were young. "Every Sunday after church we'd walk up there," said Mrs. Lane. "It was all open and a nice walk, not overgrown like it is now. There would be fishing all along the creek left by the kids. Poles made of cane just lying around." Walks in the spring were Mrs. Lane's favorites. "When the dogwoods and redbuds are blooming, that's pretty. Oh, that's so pretty. Walking up through there you want to carry all that home with you." Add the stark white blossoms of the plum trees, the blues and purples of the spiderworts and violets, and the reds and pinks of the azaleas and Cardinal flowers, and the woods become a tapestry of color.

In the fall, this view is spiced with the gold and rust-colored leaves of sweet gums and maples. In the winter, the hills of silver-gray, bare-limbed trees are dotted with the greens of cedars and pines, and the bluffs are sculptured in ice.

Any time of the year, a float through this part of the East Cadron makes you want to stop just to take it all in. The bizarre tupelo gum trees dominate the scene, standing like guards along the pools and like

Rainbow Falls

slalom poles in the rapids. They create a secluded environment similar to a Florida cypress swamp except that the water here is clear and cool.

Of the long-gone communities, legendary water holes and busy mills that are associated with Cadron Creek history, the East Fork had its share. Many more homes once stood where cattle now roam near the Lane farm. In the 1930's people started moving out in search of more secure employment, but in recent years many have been returning to the rural environment. "Used to be a lot of people lived in this country in here," said James Lane. "There was little houses just sittin' along the road that used to go to the bluff." Like most houses today in Arkansas, the older ones had no basements. "They just built them on top of the ground, just stacked filler rocks up and put their sills on them," James explained. "Then, if the house burned down or moved off and rotted, they'd just hoe the rocks and haul them off. No signs of 'em anymore."

Almost every hole—or pool—on the East Cadron has a name. "It's just something mainly for people to pinpoint spots on the creek. They must have named some of 'em years ago for some of the folks who lived near 'em—like Grey Hole. (Supposedly named after one of the Grey boys dived from a high bluff into the

deep hole and never came up.) They're called holes because they're deeper areas of water. Most of them are good fishin' holes," said James. Some of the popular holes within walking distance of the Lane home are Cedar Branch, Fish Trap, Upper Rock, Lower Rock, Dancing and Mill. Grey Hole and Blue Hole (the deepest and longest in the creek, according to farmers) are west of Highway 107, beyond the Lane farm and take out place, on a stretch of the Cadron seldom floated but often fished. Dancing Hole is just behind the Lane home. "They claim back years ago that people used to meet there and match up and party and dance, you know, right out on the creek bank. They say that's how it got its name," said James. "It's like havin' our own swimmin' area; it's so close." Mrs. Lane added: "They had a swing *way* up in the trees. Looked like they were falling from the sky. And they once had a diving board there. Now, every Sunday afternoon in the summer there are crowds at rock pool."

Although most Arkansas creeks are too low to float in the summer months, there were many times when James Lane could float a mile or more without interference from rocks and logs. "When I was younger, I used to walk up to the bluff in trunks and swim down to the bridge—just float with the current.

Myrtle Lane

ferent saw mills near the Cadron. Large rocks on the bank and in the water mark the location where the creek was forded. This spot, on a sharp bend in the creek, is one of the trickiest rapids for canoeists. "I remember goin' over to that mill in a wagon when I was a real small kid," James explained. "About the only thing I remember about the old mill was catchin' that hot meal and eatin' it—was **real** good and hot!"

Just below the Lane home and only about 200 yards from Highway 107 is Baptizing Hole, a small, shallow area close to the road. Churches from several miles around still baptize here on Sunday evenings. "That's just common with the country churches now," said James. "They have a certain place on the creek that they can get into and baptize out there. This is the main one always used up around here."

James Lane has fished many miles of the East Cadron. His favorite hole is Cedar Branch, only a short walk from his home—so near it's like having his private fishing pond. But if the fish aren't biting in Cedar Branch, James has only to move a few hundred feet to any one of several good fishing spots. "I figured the whole creek was filled with holes of fish," laughed Mrs. Lane. "I'd see the kids come off the road and they couldn't hardly walk, they'd have so many fish on the string." Fishermen are still an everyday sight on the East Cadron, floating in johnboats or eyeing the lines of several poles braced with rocks on the banks. Bass, bream and flathead or channel catfish are the most common fish caught in the creek.

Frog gigging is another common pastime in the East Fork, especially for youngsters. The best way to gig frogs, according to James who has carried many pailsful home, is to walk through the water. "You can't see the frogs from the bank. You'd make a lot more noise and scare 'em in. From the creek, you're in front of the frog because he's sittin' there facin' the water ready to jump in. You see that white belly shinin' and his eyes."

Frog gigging "used to be every Saturday night's job," said Mrs. Lane. "They'd get 25 or 30. I'd just round up a big pan full." Many Sunday dinners for the Lanes featured frog legs.

When John was just a little boy, he'd sometimes come and float between two of us all the way."

Although more mills were on the banks of the North Cadron years ago, a few were gathering places for people on the East Fork. Mill Hole was named for a saw mill and grist mill that operated about 100 yards from the creek on the south side, just downstream from Mansfield Bluff. Those living north of the creek traveled in wagons on a road that now goes through the Lane farm to take their grains to be ground at the mill. Logs also were hauled on this road to two dif-

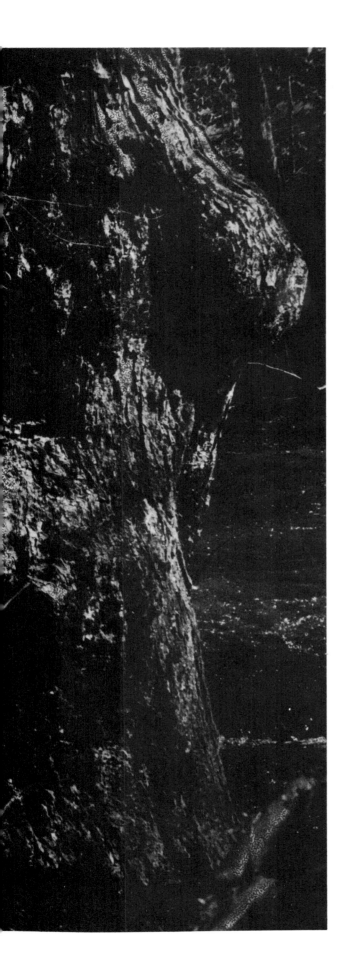

One reason James enjoys gigging once in a while is to observe things that aren't seen in the daytime. "You see most anything at night by the creek—mink, beaver, snakes, an occasional deer. Some are out in the day, but at night there's plenty of 'em."

James has speared a lot of frogs in his time, but he prefers to catch them with his hands—even at the risk of grabbing a cottonmouth which also is attracted to the light in this nocturnal setting. "I don't know why I've not been bit a dozen times. I never think anything about a snake when I'm down on the creek."

Once when the Lane brothers were fishing in their johnboat, a little water snake dropped from a branch into their boat. "I was fixin' to get him out but he ran under my seat. I saw him come out one time and started to get him but he ran back under. So, I said, if he won't bother me, I won't bother him." And the snake rode home with them.

Now and then, the Lane children brought a king snake into the house "as long as this floor lamp," shuddered Mrs. Lane. Snakes aren't her favorite pets, but she accepted them as part of her children's experiences with wild creatures. "We've had all kinds of things in here. You never knew what they'd bring from the creek."

The East Cadron provided the Lanes with another experience that James laughs about. "Oh, yea. A lot of times I'd wash in the creek. I'd be out in the summertime workin', you know, and be all sweated and dusty. Instead of gettin' in an old galvanized tub and drawin' it full of water, well, I'd just get me a bar of soap and go to the creek and take a bath. It hasn't been that long since we've had runnin' water and electricity."

Mrs. Lane laughed: "That used to be every evening! That's the way, instead of taking a bath in an old tub." And it was a lot more fun, both agreed.

The soap seemed to please the fish, too. "That soap draws the fish to you. They like it," chuckled James. "They'll just peck you to death, the little ones, you know. Be just peckin' around on the bubbles. Don't see this anymore because of modern conveniences, water in homes and pumps. Back then, we didn't have good fresh water at the house."

A few years ago, James Lane spent a short time in a part of California where people had to drive as far as 50 miles to get to a body of water to fish or swim. He was glad to get back to Cadron country. "Just to live right here—with the creek right at our back door. We really got it made if you stop to think about it," James smiled with a nod of his head. "Guess we have it lucky!" his mother said.

Mansfield Bluff

74

The Lowlands

Hardin Bridge

Leaving the hilly country of its upper reaches and spreading into the lowlands of Faulkner County, the East Cadron skims the eastern edge of Cadron Valley, with Bailey Mountain on the north and Hardin Hill on the south. Towering trees and worn, shrubless banks create a shady, spectral atmosphere where the old Clinton to Little Rock road (now county road 310) intersects the Cadron between Enola and McGinty-town. Here, the Hardin Bridge—a long, narrow iron structure—crosses high above the creek.

Old-timers have many tales about this area, mainly ghost stories about the wagon travelers. Horses, it is told, would not pass one place called "haunted ditch" at night. Although the spooky origin of the slough south of the bridge is not known, one farmer said he always heard that bandits once attacked two men in a wagon at that spot, and that the horses were run into the slough. "The men went back to the tavern (Hardin House) and told their story and ever since nobody wanted to go past that ditch," the farmer said. Why ghost stories grew from this episode is still a mystery to local residents, but the legend continues. For years, a dummy was hung from an old oak tree across the road from the slough. A few years ago the dummy appeared again, but farmers say it's just a prank by some young kids who heard the old stories.

Jacob Hardin settled in this area in 1823. During the mid-1800's, his son Jonathan Hardin and his family owned 840 acres of land west of Enola and lived on Hardin Hill overlooking the East Cadron. Their two-story dwelling, known as Hardin House, was made of hewn oak logs with large chimneys at both sides. It served as a tavern, inn and gathering place for travelers on this stage route. Local farmers contend that many wagoners stayed overnight at Hardin House so that they could pass "haunted ditch" in daylight.

Nothing remains of Hardin House; however, the Hardin family cemetery is about 100 yards off a county road on the southern edge of Hardin Hill. The flat stones marking the graves still stand, but mounds of dirt show that the grave sites have been disturbed.

"I've been up there shortly after they was dug up several years ago," recalled one area resident. "They didn't take the bodies but were looking for something—money's what everybody says. I don't know why they'd bury money."

As the pools of the East Cadron get longer and the flow slower beyond the Hardin Bridge, the country lures more coyote and squirrel hunters and fishermen than canoeists. About six miles downstream, the East Fork passes under the new Terry Bridge on Highway 287 near Linder, between Springhill and Holland. Many families named Terry farmed here years ago. Three tributaries merge into the Cadron about a half mile above the bridge: Black Fork, Big Branch and Needs Creek, all coming out of Bald Hill from the northwest. The original Terry Bridge, torn down about 30 years ago, was about one mile east of Highway 65, on the first road north of the East Cadron. The approach to the creek on this narrow road is densely overgrown, with trees close in on both sides. Mirky water and mud-splattered tree trunks tell you that this is the Cadron bottoms.

Cleared bank below Hardin Bridge

Near the mouth of the Cadron

Several clearings on the south bank mark the location of a saw mill run by Obitz and Miller in the first decade of this century. Lumber and stave bolts were sawed there. Close by is the Terry Cemetery.

"I was the one that caught the lumber that came out sawed and culled it," recalled 84-year-old Bob Fugatt who worked at the mill for about three years prior to World War I. "Kept the good parts and sacked the bad ones. They couldn't have any knots or bends in them."

Pastures and new homes now occupy this land that once was thickly wooded with white and pin oaks. "Some of the finest timber in the Cadron bottomlands that I've ever seen. Not any there anymore," said Fugatt. "They've cleaned it up. Now it's only scrub timber. I sure did hate to see that happen." The woods have been cleared for decades, but their passing seems recent to Fugatt who hunted and walked through them for many happy years.

This part of the Cadron, free of rapids and rocks, was excellent for transporting lumber on the slow, smooth current. "I've seen people go above the Terry Bridge and cut logs, haul them out to the banks, tie them with short chains with hooks in each end. When the Cadron got up, deep enough, they'd float them to Gleason where there was the biggest saw mill in this

country. The company that ran that mill were the ones who had the logs cut," explained Fugatt. "Men got on log rafts—had to guide them along the banks. Dangerous. Sometimes they'd lose some (men)."

Bob Fugatt knew many miles of the East Cadron. "I've done a lot of hunting over in that bottom. That's where I used to go 'coon hunting. Had a lot of fun there. Good memories. Was good hunting ducks and squirrels over there, too. Kill all you wanted."

Like her father, Foye Mae Fugatt Bane of Conway found many pleasant days on the Cadron. "Went to the creek to hunt all the time. Oh, I **loved** to hunt, mostly squirrels. Enjoyed myself over there."

Although farm work kept the Fugatt family busy, they all found time to spend on the Cadron: "That's the only place we had to go swimming and fishing," Fugatt said. "We went there often." Only Dunn Hill separates the Cadron from the Fugatt home, about a half mile south of the creek. The baptizing place for people of that area was at the saw mill-bridge site. Fugatt and his wife Elsie were baptized there more than 60 years ago.

The East Fork takes on an entirely different aspect as it continues past the old Terry Bridge area through the bottom lands, winding about 12 miles through marshes and farms, row cropped mainly in soybeans and rice. North Cadron Ridge provides a wooded shield on the right side, but open farm land accompanies the creek on the left as it passes under Highways 65 and 25 and twists its way to its junction with the North Fork on the Faulkner-Conway County border. Through this lowland region, fishermen take to the widening Cadron in motor boats, a sight one seldom sees in other parts of the creek.

A short distance upstream from the mouth of the Cadron, where Highway 64 now crosses the creek, was the Gleason and Western Lumber Mill. It occupied part of the land which now is the community of Gleason. Before the state highway was built, a railroad went into the bottoms to get lumber for the mill. Menifee House, the mill superintendent, owned much of the land in the area and black laborers lived at his lumber camp in tents while clearing the land. The town of Menifee, a few miles west in Conway County, was named for House.

An excelsior mill, built in the late 1890's between the railroad and the north side of the Cadron, made wood shavings. The cement foundation and an underground storage area are still intact. Steam boilers ran both the saw mill and excelsior mill. Amidst the sounds of screeching saws, chugging trains and hissing steam boilers, Victor Halter and his buddies played on the boardwalks and remains of a group of buildings once occupied by mill employees.

Bob Fugatt

Remains of excelsior mill
near mouth of Cadron Creek

80

"The homes were built on pilings but were already abandoned when I was a kid," the 78-year-old Halter said. Although he lived in Conway, Halter spent much time on the Cadron near where his father farmed. On these trips he passed a whiskey still "set out in the middle of Flag Pond, a swamp where Highway 64 is before you get to Gleason. They built it out on the pond to keep the revenuers from getting to it."

The old Cadron settlement was part of Halter's stomping grounds. "We'd find musket balls there. I must have picked up hundreds of them over the years as a kid. We'd shoot them in bean flips, throw them at each other, did a lot of things with them for fun. People made them out of lead."

Best remembered by Halter, however, is the excitement he and his friends found on the Cadron. "We had homemade boats, with oar locks, and went up and down the Cadron fishing and frog hunting. Also went wild boar hunting up there. Why, we even courted by the creek. We'd listen to the whippoor-wills all night," he laughed.

Gathering nuts was another occasion for fun in Halter's younger days. "Every year in the fall we'd go up on the Cadron and get bushels of pecans. Also were a lot of scaley bark hickory nut trees there. But all those trees are gone now. All the old timber has been cleared out. Back then, saw mills were all over, by the creek and in the town," he said.

"There were lots of roads back then. You could get any place by the creek. In the 1920's, people got around. In the old Model-T's. We had all our picnics on the creek. We'd net fish and have a fish fry," recalled Halter. "We always had something to do on the Cadron."

For more than a century, Cadron Creek has been an intimate part of the lives of many people—from the economy provided by the early mills, whose wheels the creek turned; to the meals of fish caught in its pools; to the gatherings on the banks for picnics, swimming and baptisms; to the recreational pleasures of canoeists and hunters. Much of the satisfaction and excitement has been found in the intangibles along its route—the beauty and the inspiration of freedom. Over the years, the shared sights, sounds and uses of the Cadron have strengthened friendships with others and with the creek.

Epilogue

More than 10 years ago, the Soil Conservation Service proposed a plan to place 23 earthen structures on Cadron Creek and its tributaries. Due to pressure from various organizations, the number of proposed dams has been reduced to 14. The original goals for the project were conservation land treatment, drainage, municipal and industrial water supply, flood prevention, and fish and wildlife and recreation. Drainage since has been omitted from the list, and flood prevention has been the SCS's major thrust in recent years. Opponents to the project realize the flooding problem of the Cadron but are not convinced that constructing dams will stop flooding. Specifically, the issue being argued is how to reduce flood damage in the lower floodplain of the watershed. Alternatives are being sought in lieu of dams. A decision on the project is pending in legislative water resources committees.

About five years ago, the Ozark Society decided to publish books on various endangered Arkansas streams in hopes of exposing the scenic, geological, historical, fish and wildlife, educational and cultural values and of emphasizing the need to preserve our water resources in their natural state. The *Illinois River* by Ken Smith was the first in this series, published in 1977. *Cadron Creek: A Photographic Narrative* is the second endeavor. Previously, in 1967, the Ozark Society published Smith's *Buffalo River Country*.

When the Ozark Society asked if I were interested in doing a book on Cadron Creek, shortly after my arrival in Arkansas, I accepted the challenge without ever having seen the creek. I felt, however, that if the Society had hoped to eulogize Cadron Creek in book form, the creek must have something to offer.

In the following four years, I've canoed and walked all but a few miles of the Cadron—in all seasons—experiencing its wildness and serenity, its pristine, unspoiled beauty. I've seen herons and cottonmouths, trout lilies and beavers, massive ice columns and water-stained caves. I've survived churning rapids in high water and dragged canoes through shallow shoals and water weeds. I've welcomed the spray of boiling haystacks in the hot summer and felt the cold wet chill in winter after my canoe was overturned by the incredible power of the creek's current.

It didn't take long to find that the charm of knowing the Cadron lay in being a part of the rocks, the ripples and every living thing in its environment. Indeed, Cadron Creek does have much to offer. As I became more involved in this project, I soon found myself and my friends referring to the Cadron as my creek. After listening to people who have lived for years with the Cadron at their back door, I found that they, too, called the Cadron their creek. It's this kind of relationship that the Cadron reveals—closeness, uniqueness, enchantment, appeal.

But the focus on the Cadron is more than a description of its natural landscape. The people and their bond with the creek have helped to shape the cultural landscape that has added a humanistic aspect to the creek and its environment. When the early settlers arrived in the Arkansas Territory in the 1800's, the Cadron was a means of transportation. As settlements grew upstream and along its tributaries, the creek became an important factor in the economy of the communities. Grist mills, saw mills, felly mills, stave bolt mills, excelsior mills and whiskey stills operated along its route. People gathered at the creek for baptisms, social events, relaxation and news. The Cadron was a water source for farm animals and a habitat and food resource for many species of fauna like beavers, deer, squirrels, bears, ducks and turkeys—so important to the subsistence of the pioneers.

In the past 30 years, technology and mechanization brought progress and a change in the daily routine of the people and their communities. Cadron Creek, however, has changed little since the days of the early settlers and still remains an influence in the lives of those living nearby.

Floating Guide To Cadron Creek

Although most of Cadron Creek is floatable, four stretches on both the North and East Forks are the most popular and offer some challenging runs and exciting scenery. They are the Iron Bridge (North Guy) to Pinnacle Springs; Pinnacle Springs to Highway 65; Highway 65 to Highway 295—all on the North Fork; and Highway 36 to Highway 107 on the East Fork.

The best season is from mid-March to June; however, canoeing is becoming an almost year-around recreation on the Cadron as more and more canoeists have been floating from September to mid-November and even during the winter and summer months.

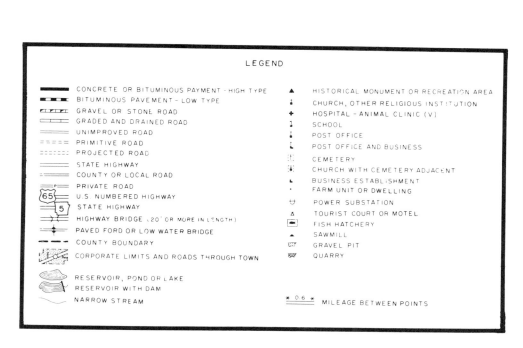

LEGEND

▬▬▬	CONCRETE OR BITUMINOUS PAVMENT - HIGH TYPE	▲	HISTORICAL MONUMENT OR RECREATION AREA
▬□▬□	BITUMINOUS PAVEMENT - LOW TYPE	⌁	CHURCH, OTHER RELIGIOUS INSTITUTION
▬▬▬	GRAVEL OR STONE ROAD	✚	HOSPITAL - ANIMAL CLINIC (V)
▭▭▭	GRADED AND DRAINED ROAD	⌐	SCHOOL
═══	UNIMPROVED ROAD	⌁	POST OFFICE
=====	PRIMITIVE ROAD	⌐	POST OFFICE AND BUSINESS
::::::	PROJECTED ROAD	⊡	CEMETERY
═══	STATE HIGHWAY	⊡	CHURCH WITH CEMETERY ADJACENT
════	COUNTY OR LOCAL ROAD	◣	BUSINESS ESTABLISHMENT
══	PRIVATE ROAD	·	FARM UNIT OR DWELLING
(65)	U.S. NUMBERED HIGHWAY	⊔	POWER SUBSTATION
(5)	STATE HIGHWAY	△	TOURIST COURT OR MOTEL
→→→	HIGHWAY BRIDGE (20' OR MORE IN LENGTH)	▬	FISH HATCHERY
→✚→	PAVED FORD OR LOW WATER BRIDGE	▲	SAWMILL
▬ ▬ ▬	COUNTY BOUNDARY	⊠	GRAVEL PIT
∷∷∷	CORPORATE LIMITS AND ROADS THROUGH TOWN	⊠	QUARRY
⬭	RESERVOIR, POND OR LAKE		
⬭	RESERVOIR WITH DAM		
∿	NARROW STREAM	* 0.6 *	MILEAGE BETWEEN POINTS

86

North Fork

Headwaters to Highway 124

Location: Southeastern Van Buren County.
Length: 15 miles; 5-6 paddling hours.
Put in: Bridge on county road, north of Gravesville.
Take out: Highway 124 bridge.
Shuttle length: 6 miles (15 minutes). West on gravel road to paved road. South to Highway 124. East to bridge.
Classification: Families, beginners.
Camping: None
Difficulties: None.

This upper float is not popular because of many long pools and few rapids. It is suitable, however, for an easy day float with many places to stop and fish. The first few miles are the most intriguing because the Cadron is narrow and winding, and trees reaching across the creek conceal it from the sun. This stretch cuts through White Oak Mountain. One interesting feature is passing by the junction of the North and West Forks at Gooch Bend, about five miles from the put in point. From here on, the creek widens and low bluffs begin to appear amidst open pastures and woods. Ample parking is available at the Gravesville bridge, but parking space is limited at the take out place

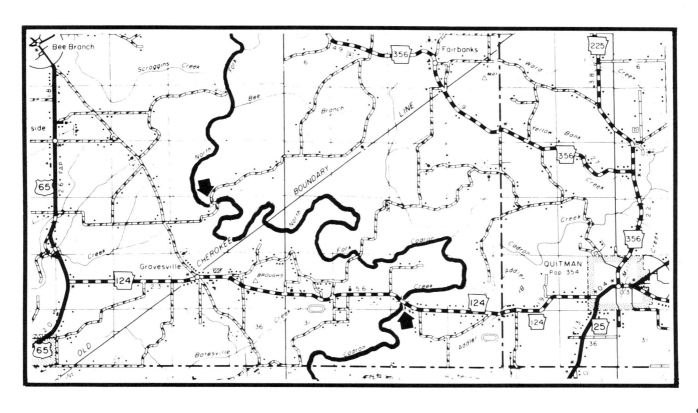

Highway 124 to Iron Bridge (North Guy)

Location: Southeastern Van Buren and Northcentral Faulkner Counties.
Length: 6 miles; 3-4 paddling hours.
Put in: Highway 124 bridge.
Take out: Iron bridge.
Shuttle length: 4 miles (15 minutes). One mile west on Highway 124, left on county road at church to iron bridge.
Classification: Families, beginners.
Camping: Yes, at take out point.
Difficulties: None.

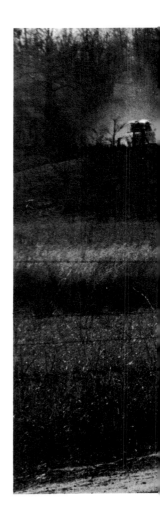

This is a good stretch for those learning to canoe or desiring to take time to fish. Kennimer, King and Stillhouse Branches enter the Cadron as it flows to the southeast of Batesville Mountain. At the take out spot, the clearing on the south bank is sufficient room for tents and parking. At the bridge, rocks left from a dam mark the site of the old Hartwick grist mill. There is limited parking at the Highway 124 bridge.

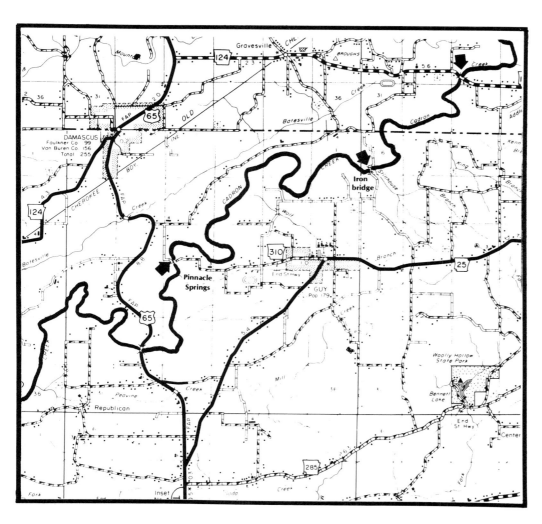

Road leading to iron bridge (Old Hartwick mill place)

Iron Bridge to Pinnacle Springs

Location: Northwestern Faulkner County.
Length: 10 miles; 3-4 paddling hours.
Put in: Iron bridge (North Guy).
Take out: Pinnacle Springs picnic area (west of Guy).
Shuttle length: 8 miles (25 minutes). South on county road to Highway 25. West to county road 310 to creek.
Classification: Families, beginners.
Camping: Yes, at both ends.
Difficulties: Narrow chutes close to bluffs, willow bushes.

This stretch has been gaining in popularity as canoeists discover more intense scenery in the higher moss-covered bluffs, rocky banks, wooded hills and waterfalls. Batesville Mountain lies to the north. Wolf Branch enters from the southeast about six miles downstream. Plenty of space is available for parking at both ends.

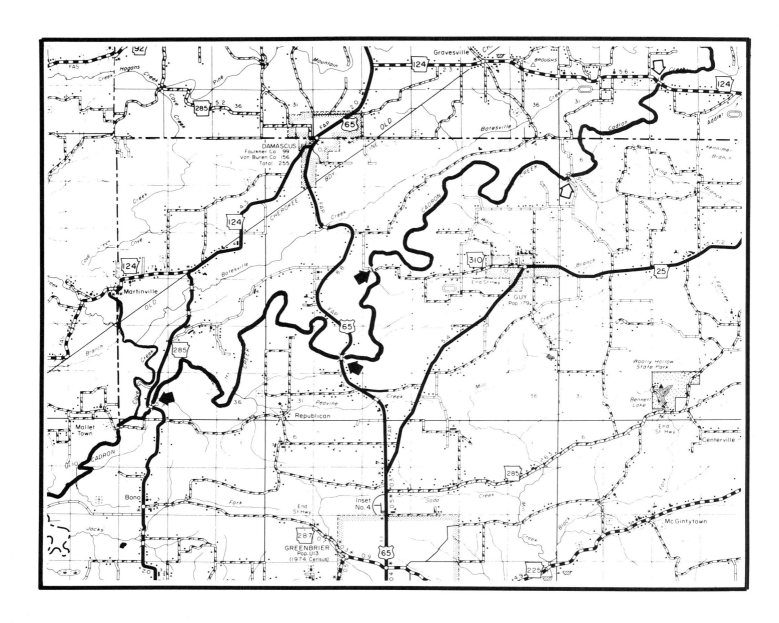

Pinnacle Springs to Highway 65

Location: Northwestern Faulkner County.

Length: 3 miles; 1-2 paddling hours.

Put in: Pinnacle Springs picnic area (west of Guy).

Take out: Highway 65 bridge (steep ascent).

Shuttle length: 10 miles (40 minutes). East on county road 310. South on Highway 25 to first county road. West to Highway 65. North to bridge.

Classification: Families, beginners.

Camping: Yes, at put in place. (Woolly Hollow State Park is 10 miles—south on Highway 65, then east on Highway 285).

Difficulties: Few rapids on short curves, willow bushes.

Winding away from Batesville Mountain, this is the shortest and most popular stretch on the North Fork. Many canoeists continue past Highway 65 to Highway 285, a full day's float. The west pinnacle at Pinnacle Points Gap (about one-half mile from the put in spot) is easily climbed and gives an inspiring view of the hilly terrain cut through by the Cadron. Owl's Home bluff and Bear's Cave also are attractions. A rock quarry is south of the creek near the take out place. Plenty of parking is available at Pinnacle Springs, but there is limited space on Highway 65, a busy north-south artery.

Highway 65 to Highway 285

Location: Northwestern Faulkner County.
Length: 11 miles; 4-5 paddling hours.
Put in: Highway 65 bridge (difficult descent).
Take out: Highway 285 bridge.
Shuttle length: 14 miles (25 minutes). North on Highway 65 to Highway 124. West to Highway 285. South to bridge. **Or** 8 miles (40 minutes). South on Highway 65 to first county road. West through Republican community to Highway 285. North to bridge.
Classification: Beginners, intermediates.
Camping: None (Woolly Hollow State Park is 10 miles—south on Highway 65, then east on Highway 285).
Difficulties: Churning rapids close to bluffs, curves, Rock of Gibraltar on fast bend, willow bushes.

This is the most challenging float trip on the North Cadron. In high water, waves reaching to four feet are capable of swamping canoes. The creek forks at various places, with alternate channels floatable when water is up. The creek heads northwest to Batesville Mountain which forms its high right bank for several miles before it heads south to Rosin Hill. The long, steep bluffs are the highest and longest on the North Fork. Limited parking is available at both ends.

Cove Creek: One of the Cadron's largest tributaries, Cove Creek enters about one mile beyond the Highway 285 bridge. Some canoe this creek from Martinville (five miles northwest) to the Cadron and either paddle upstream to take out at the Highway 285 bridge or head one mile downstream to the Mallettown Bridge, just across the Conway County line.

East Fork

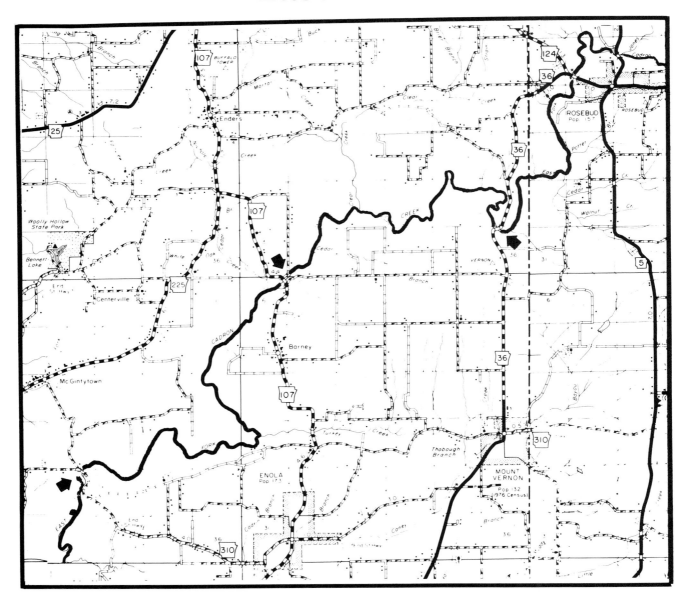

Highway 36 to Highway 107

Location: Northeastern Faulkner County

Length: 8 miles; 4-5 paddling hours.

Put in: Highway 36 bridge (steep, rocky descent; barbed wire fence to cross).

Take out: Highway 107 bridge.

Shuttle length: 5 miles (20 minutes). South on Highway 36 to first county road. West to Highway 107. North across bridge.

Classification: Intermediate.

Camping: None (Woolly Hollow State Park is 9 miles north on Highway 107 to Highway 285; 5 miles south on county road 285).

Difficulties: Swift currents winding around tupelo gum trees, willow bushes, logs across creek, rapids and rocks on narrow turns.

This is the most popular stretch on the East Fork—and the most intriguing of the entire Cadron because of the tupelo gum trees scattered throughout the water. The creek changes abruptly in water level and style—from calm movement along creekside pastures in Molly Bottoms to tumbling rapids every few hundred feet and many straggly channels. In low water, floating is not advisable because of many rocky shoals. In high water, high waves can swamp canoes and tupelos in the path of the fast current can be canoe wreckers.

Special attractions are Star Bluff and Buzzard's Roost just before Clear Creek enters from Beckette Mountain on the right; Mansfield Bluff and Rainbow Falls, about a half hour from the take out place. Little parking is available at the put in spot, but plenty of off-road parking is available at the Highway 107 bridge.

Highway 107 to Hardin Bridge

Location: Northeastern Faulkner County.
Length: 10 miles; 5-6 paddling hours.
Put in: Highway 107 bridge.
Take out: Hardin Bridge on county road 310.
Shuttle length: 14 miles (40 minutes). South
   on Highway 107 to county road 310 in Enola.
   West to bridge.
Classification: Families, beginners.
Camping: None.
Difficulties: None.

Flowing adjacent to White Oak Mountain on the north for the first few miles, this stretch is floated more by fishermen than by canoeists because of the many long pools and slower water, especially near the end as the creek enters the lowland area. Blue Hole, said to be the deepest on the Cadron, is about two miles from Highway 107. Plenty of off-road parking is available at both ends of this stretch.

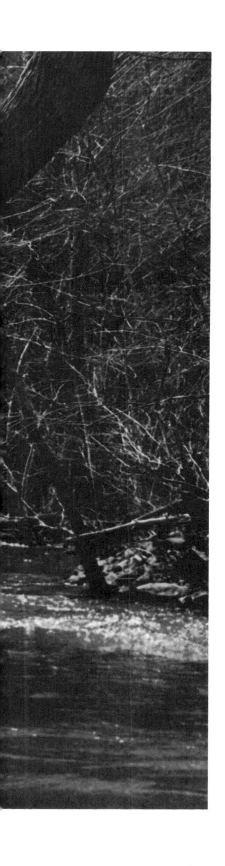

LIL JUNAS is a photojournalist with a background in college sports information, newspaper reporting and photographing, university teaching and freelancing for magazines and other publications. She has photographed throughout the United States, Mexico and Canada and in Central Asia where she covered American and Canadian mission projects in Nepal, India, Pakistan and Afghanistan.

An avid canoeist and outdoorsperson, the native Pennsylvanian has tent-camped in all states on mainland USA and in Canada and the Yukon. She spent three years as a newspaper photographer within 10 miles of the Cadron Creek watershed. She was the Arkansas News Photographer of the Year for 1978.